WHAT'S YOUR PROBLEM?

What's Your Problem?

A collection of poems by pupils and students of
the Guy's Evelina Hospital School

Edited by Wendy French and Clive Niall
Cover design by Samantha
Illustrations by the authors
Additional illustrations by Daniel

Rockingham Press

First published 2004
by The Rockingham Press
11 Musley Lane,
Ware, Herts SG12 7EN

**A catalogue record of this book is available
from the British Library**

ISBN 1-904851-05-3

Lottery Grants for Local Groups

*AWARDS
FOR ALL*

Printed in Great Britain by
Biddles Limited
Kings Lynn

CONTENTS

FOREWORD

What happens when a young person attends a hospital school? Many people don't know that hospital schools even exist and yet sick children and adolescents of school age have a statutory right to education.

Aren't these young people simply too ill to carry on with their education? Certainly many think that the focus should be on simply getting better, as if the rest of life becomes suspended in the meantime. But continuity is important. Absence from school or college life, missing educational experiences and friendships do not aid recovery.

This school has been in existence as long as the NHS itself and over the years we have played an essential role in continuing the education of paediatric inpatients, bringing some "normality" during their illness. We endeavour to provide a curriculum which is meaningful in a hospital situation and has relevance in the outside world so that young people, and others, know they matter.

I am really pleased to introduce this book of our students' poems. Not only because it ably demonstrates the obvious – that feelings and thoughts and abilities continue and develop through illness – but also because it will be terrifically exciting for a young person to see their work printed in a commercial form.

And it's a great read!

Thanks are due to teacher Clive Niall, who persevered with the concept of this project, and poet Wendy French who played a large part in its realisation. Thanks also to John Alderson, a local graphic designer who worked with us during Big Arts Week to produce some newspaper graphics included here.

Thanks to Daniel too who, although he didn't write a poem for this collection, did provide a number of illustrations at short notice.

We are grateful that this book was made possible by a grant from Awards for All.

Alan Chapman
Headteacher

My Garden of Earthly Delights

In my garden of earthly delights I shall put the warmth of a summer's day.

In my garden of earthly delights I shall put the joy of a child and the comfort of a mother's hug.

In my garden of earthly delights I shall put the breeze of the Atlantic and the sight of the Himalayas.

In my garden of earthly delights I shall put a crystal clear day followed by a spectral night sky.

In my garden of earthly delights I shall put the karma of good and the karma of bad, as this is a garden made on a balanced land.

Giuseppe

THE MOON CAT

The moon cat lives on top of the moon. It comes out quietly
in the afternoon.
It glows so bright all through the night. I hear it
purring and curling up tight.
You could say *what a beautiful sight.*
The cat moon smiles and curls up to sleep and dreams
of people diving into the sea that's deep.
The cat moon's so friendly. The owner is the man in the moon.
The man in the moon loves his moon cat, yellow with whiskers
and silver cheeks.
They stay out at night days, months, years and weeks.
The cat moon is scratching the soft yellow moon
and I hope that I'll see them both soon.

The man and his cat shine into my room and I wish, I wish I could
fly in a rocket zooooooooooooooooooom.

Lee

Jungle

Jungles are the home of tigers
Umbrella-like enormous leaves
Night-time bats fly over water
Gorillas are camouflaged in the dark
Lions are kings of the jungle
Elephants gnaw at the barks of trees.

Kieran, Junior

THE MONKEY

I am approaching,
            swinging through the trees,

I stop and pick up a fruit and eat it,
            the birds chatter…. And I swing on,

faster and faster and up and down,
            below me I pass the thundering waterfall,

red and blue flowers by the bank
                  but watch out…. here comes a tiger
            coming to drink.

            The day is hot and I stop and sit in a tree,
grab a banana, eat it.
Relax.

Mary

THE GOAT BY THE SEA

In my mind I can see a river shining –
green, yellow and red hills –
in the distance there is a volcano,
a girl is playing with the trees.
The house is glowing and I would like to enter it.
The goat by itself, looking for more goats.
Maybe I could go swimming in the sea
with the goat and splash and splash

                    and splash it all around

Fahmida

MY SNAKE

I love my snake with an S because

He's slippery
He's slimy
He's slug like
He's scaly
He's sensible
He's scientific
He's sharp
He's shady
He's shabby
He's severe
He's shiny
He's shy
He's silent
He's super

Joseph

Snake girl

Her pink snakes hissing at each other.
Her one eye blinking every few seconds.
Her purple skin smooth on her frail body.
Her green dress hanging loosely at her sides.
Her arms long and slim, her hands fingerless.

A bunch of pink and purple snakes for her feet slivering
smoothly over the rough atmosphere.
Her antennae picking up sound from over 5 miles away.
When she is angry she sends snakes down to the earth
crashing on people's heads.
But when she is happy she blesses every one who is
doing good.

Chloe Barton

PARROT

Junior's parrot is grey and red
It eats snakes and flies through the jungle
Junior's Dad starts looking for it
When he finds it he takes it back home
Junior closes the window.

Junior's parrot

On the Beach

On the beach at the end of the day
I can smell you
The crawling crab pinches you on the back
OW
I see the picnic lunch and I feel the pain
I eat my snack and go for a swim

Sam

Island Poem

My eyes opened up to a desert beach,
I climbed out of my boat.
Cut my feet on the jagged rocks.

I staggered to the nearest shelter,
frightened and lonely,
Absorbing the island's towering mountain.

That night I scurried to a cave.
It was a nightmare,
I just couldn't sleep.

I woke up to the sound of running pigs,
men sprinting after them,
perching spears on their shoulders.

I soon got used to the way of island life.
Minutes became long hours,
Hours became dragging days.

I wrote a message in a bottle,
praying it would be found.
But no one replied.

I just have to wait now.
It's been two years today
since I got shipwrecked on this island.
I'm still very scared.

Claire

MY PRINCESS

I want to leave this island

      A princess to come and rescue me

Wearing a long purple dress

        She'll be riding in a boat of many colours.

Patterned. She comes.

There's been a storm, lightening and heavy rain.

The sea is like crashing cars.

        My princess comes.

Mohammed

THE INVITATION OF FRIENDS

I invite you to come home and drink blackcurrant with me.

        I invite you to come and taste Ben and Jerry's
        ice cream with me.

I invite you to come and watch the Simpsons with me.

        I invite you to eat fish on Bournemouth
        beach with me.

I invite you to come and *parlez-francais avec moi.*

        I invite you to ride at Alton Towers with me.

I invite you to paint the town red with me.

        I invite you to gallop the sands with me.

Naomi and Mohammed

THE BLUE WE SEE

The blue we see is in the sky

The blue we see is in our eyes

The blue we see is at the sea-side

The blue we see is near the tide

Naomi

THE SEA

I like to go to the sea-side because I can splash in the water.
I can swim to the end of the sea.

There'll be sharks, jellyfish, squids and octopus.
Dolphins, eels, whales, flatfish, shiny fish, flying fish,
sword fish, hammerheads and white sharks.

I like throwing stones and hear them go plop.
I'd like to skim stones but I can't.
I love the sea breeze.

We go on boats and see dolphins, mummies and babies.
I like the frequency of the waves on a hot summer day.
The waves and the waves and the waves.

Jamie, Zoe

THINGS THAT FALL FROM THE SKY

Damp furred cats and dogs spread-eagled
Plunging wet rain
Diving men from a cloud
A surprise
Slow leaves from the trees
Bread from a window
Cherubs with wings
Arcing footballs missing the goal
Tinkling angels toppled from grace.

Sam

DOB

Dream On Baby

Dogs Often Bark

Don't Offer Biscuits

Diamonds On Broadway

Desperate Over Ball

Dear Oliver Bromwell

Dog Over Board

Don't Open Books

Drink Only Beer

Drive On Boat

Drunk On Board

Dinosaurs Often Bite

Duck Opens Beak

James

AUTUMN COLOURS

RED AS THE BRIGHT BERRIES

YELLOW AS THE MORNING SUN

GREEN AS THE TALL GRASS

BLUE AS THE FRESH SKY

BROWN AS THE BARK OF A TREE

BLACK AS THE DARK BERRIES

Sade

RED

Red is like blood

Red is like tomatoes

Red is like love

Red is like a ruby

Red is like a robin's chest

Red is a danger sign

Naomi

MORNING

It's late morning and the mid-day sun
gleams through the window.
In my topsy-turvy bedroom I feel
the warmth touch my face.
Outside I hear cheery chattering of people passing by.
The mirror reflects my face and clouds are pushed away
by the sun's strength. From the café below smells
from today's menu waft up. The blue jug contains cool water
and as I drink I spot a loose piece of red thin thread
on the rugless floor.

I am happy today and my sandals fit well.
Summer dresses float in the breeze.

Sandra, a mother

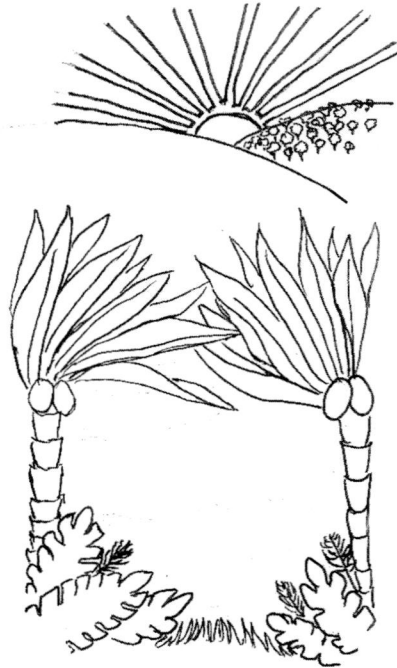

IN MY GHOST BOX

In my ghost box I shall put the chill of an empty room,

the smell of ghostly cigarette smoke

and the brush of the witch's broomstick through my hair.

In my ghostbox I shall put the smell of damp earth from the freshly dug grave,

the terrifying green eyes of a rat in the dark

and its teeth bared in its grinning mouth.

In my ghostbox I shall put the tickle of a spider creeping up my back,

the sound of the wind howling in the hospital corridors

and the dancing skeleton.

In my ghostbox I shall put the rattle of chains around the tortured ghost,

the shiver of bats in the moonlight

and lightning striking the castle on the edge of the mountain.

Anon.

IN MY GHOSTBOX

In my ghost box I shall put the chill of an empty room,
the small black-tongued dog that barks and bites,
and the knocking of the skeleton under my bed.

In my ghost box I shall put the cloud of white-hot anger
circling the globe,
the freezing breath of crows on dead trees,
and the rustling of mice in the night.

In my ghost box I shall put the silver-fanged serpent slithering
under the door,
the shadow of a huge hand on the floor,
and the blood dripping fast down the wall.

In my ghost box I shall put the tickle of a spider sleeping
in my eyebrow,
the shark sleeping in its tank,
and the fish nibbling my toes.

Rachel

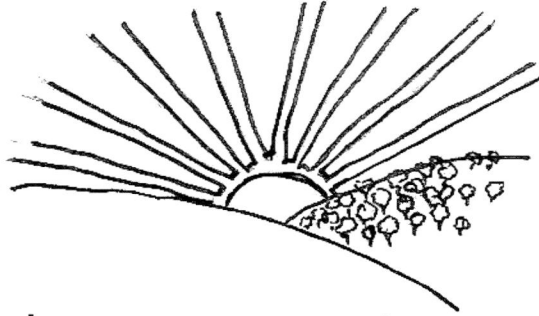

the rise of the butterfly

I've been through a lot
it hurts to think
in ink
today I'm getting stronger
a butterfly
rising to the sun

Marissa

TIMBO NURSES

Beverley

Brendan

Timbo nurses are lovely,

I like them very much.

Mala, Beverley, Carol, Pernille,

Brendan, Suzan and Hannah.

Oh, what a friendly group.

Nice and kind they are,

Unless Beverley is going bonkers,

Really, really bonkers.

She makes us laugh

Every time she does something

SILLY.

By Fahmida

WHAT AM I?

I am a light

A bright light

That flutters in the wind

I breathe the air that you all breathe

And give it back unclean

I am something

Something bright at night

When you see me you see danger

I am a crackle in the wind

I am a rage a great rage

Dying to escape

But when it's calm and everything's settles

I will simmer in the night

Slowly

Slowly

I am gone until tomorrow night

When someone will build me

So so high I rage through the night

Jermaine

MOHAMMED'S BAD DAY

I am speaking my mind but not very kind.

I am mad I am cross and feeling at a loss.

I want to punch and crunch at the boss.

Mohammed

MADNESS

It's so quiet alone in the dark room,
the stench and atmosphere is full of doom and gloom.
Trying to escape but they pull me back with a tug,
pinning me down and giving me the next dose of drugs.

I'm no criminal, nor am I a thief,
then why am I here? And when am I going to leave?
The food is horrible, especially when it comes to tea,
I wonder when my hero will come and save me.
This place I'm staying is all full of sadness.

Is it because we are all full of madness?

Warsame

FROM SOMEONE TO no one

By vampyra

unsafe

SCARED

TO

safe

Room To Noon

Rocket

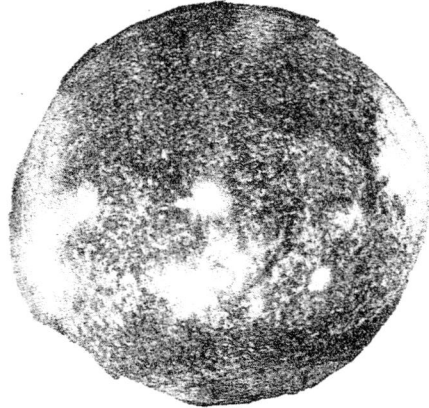

on revenge

CHANGE

I feel sick and sad and have to say
The weather is getting worse
And I'm worried about the volcano.
I am looking.

The clock is changing time
In this big city on one particular
Summer evening.
But there are colours.

Sam

What I Like and Feel and All About Me

My name is James
James as can be
I like reading books
    – History.
This is how I feel:
Happy happy as can be
Sad sad as can be
Worry worry as can be

This was written on 4th November 2003, at 3 o'clock
in the afternoon at the Bloomfield Clinic.

James

MY ANGER

Dragging of nails on surfaces
      Imagine darkness leaking
Sharpness of finger nails

Double decker exploding
      Big Ben crashing

Giuseppe

SCARED

I feel scared all the time.
I'm scared of other people's opinions of me
and how they see me.
I feel sick
tired
tense
My mind jumped ship two weeks ago
and hasn't returned since.
I doubt it ever will.
I'm scared of myself.

Rob

FRESH AIR

And the sky was blue
like a river
And the people were homeless

And the people were looking
and seeing
And at home I eat sugar cane

And I love to cut the sugar from the
tree
And the sky was blue like a river

Luke

THE JOURNEY

I have come

The music was good. It overwhelmed my emotion
And that was a good thing
It was very loud. The audience clapped
And that was a good thing

And it rose like an avalanche falling down off of a mountain

I have settled
And that was a good thing

When the play was finished we went outside

And the wind blew right upon my face

I have seen
And that was a good feeling.

Sean

GO AND OPEN THE DOOR

Go and open the door you may find
my friend with tears rolling down her face

Go and open the door and you may find
the rain hitting the floor

Go and open the door and you may find
my cousin with his best mate

Go and open the door and you may find
a stranger

At least if you open the door…

Samantha

SUPERMARKET SYMPHONY

Shuffling shoppers shove selfishly or solemnly into the store
The bakery bulges with buns, baguettes and bagels
Fingers have fun fiddling with fresh, frozen or fast food
Dairy delights and dozens of dips on delicious display
Colourful, crunchy confectionery is wrapped in crinkly crispy
coverings
Still and sparkling spring waters silently standing on shelves
As tired trolleys trundle towards the tapping tills

Snowsfields Group

I PLAY MUSIC IN THE MIDDLE OF THE NIGHT

I play music in the middle of the night
because
it brings back memories
I can't sleep
it keeps the vampires at bay
revenge for next door's chiming clock
the CD won't allow itself to be played at any other time
the bats like to join in.

Gloria, Ruemu, Sean

FRESH AIR

Yesterday I left the old miserable hospital,
went out for a breath of fresh air
to the theatre.

I am on a journey to America
it attracts me – and so do the girls.
There are bright colourful costumes
and the sound of drums.

I'll be travelling by plane
with nice cold champagne.
After the show there is
the warm dark sky

        and Indian music.

Ruemu

LONDON

London Eye green yellow at night
boats going down the river
boats haunting
Eye going round
sun setting
the Eye always going
Big Ben
Houses of Parliament
boats chugging
love not much of it
too many people on my back
hungry for more power
where is the love
it starts to rain
Eye

Ben

CITY

2

country

side

KNOCK DOWN GINGER

Walking up the street, looking for a blue front door
I stop and find it and wonder, should I play Knock Down Ginger?

I know the person who lives behind the door
but will she take it as a joke?

I'm not sure.

I take a step closer,
two steps back.

I reach for the bell, hand wavering an inch
before the button. I still don't know what to do next.

I push my index finger on the button and hear
the ring echo throughout the house.

Quick, I think. Run.

but I don't. The thought doesn't reach my feet
                                          quickly enough.

Freeze. Can't move.
Hello, is all I can say.

Sarah, Student Nursery Nurse

Me, Myself, I

If I were a car I would be a BMW 360
fast sporty dark
black mysteries
gangsters' car
clean looking
but dirty

Ben

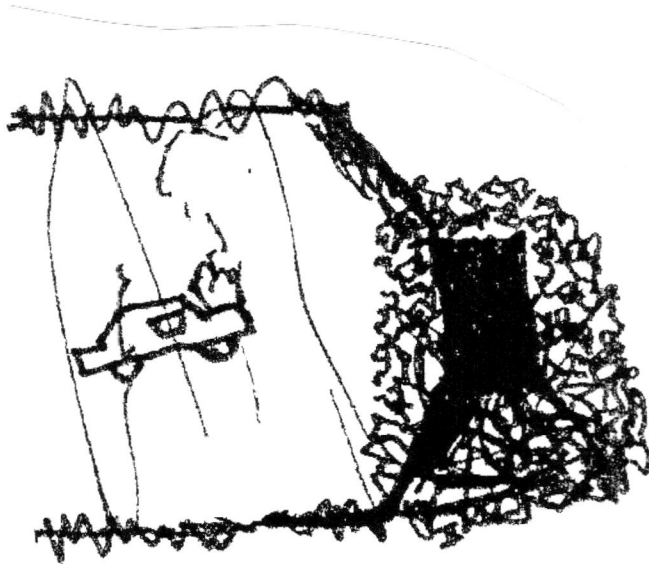

I USED TO BE

I used to be a cow
But now I'm a jacket.

I used to be a tree
But now I'm a chair.

I used to live on the earth
But now I'm on someone's plate.

I used to be a bird
But now I'm in a pillow.

I used to be on an elephant
But now I'm a necklace.

I used to be a home
But now I'm just a shell.

Mary

Happy tock
Homesick talk
I felt tock
Angry talk
Tongue-dry
Angry-tock-talk
    Very angry
Tock tock talk

Newton

A FLOWER

If I were a flower I would be like a bluebell
blue and slender, blooming in spring.
Bringing dark woods alive with colour
after the dull, grey winter.

Anon.

CITY SCENE

Arachnids agitating fearful arachnophobes
Buses bustling through Bond Street
Cabs creeping cautiously to avoid causing catastrophes
Dirty drunks disturbing the peace
Emergencies on the escalator at Elephant and Castle
Flamboyant fire engines flying through the streets
Golf sales…going going gone
Houses huddled like the homeless around a fire
Indulging in ice creams under an indigo sky
Jaywalkers jog drastically avoiding jugglers
Kind kids finding Kodak moments down the King's Road
Lollipop ladies leap lightly
Marvellous mechanics move to Milton Keynes
Newton nips noisily to new places
Oriental oranges rolled over the Oval
Police patrolling Peckham pubs
Queens request acquaintances in Queensway
Ruth runs rarely in Regent Street
Southwest trains slide sluggishly through the suburbs
Thousands of travellers trundling through the terminals
University undergraduates urge u-turn on tuition fees
Victoria vanishes in Vauxhall Vectra
William Wallace wanders through Waterloo
Foxes exit boxes at Xmas
Youngsters yodelling outside Yates'
Zany zoologists zip across the zebra crossings.

Snowsfields group

SOUTH LONDON GIRL

My name is Amy
How do you do?
I got blue eyes
And blonder hair too
I got a little nose
But a very big mouth
I'm a London girl
And I live in the South

Amy

Ta'amiya
(bean burgers from Sudan)

250g cooked chickpeas
2 tablespoons parsley
1 small onion
1 and a half tablespoons of ground cumin
1 and a half tablespoons of ground coriander
1 egg
2 tablespoons chili powder
half a teaspoon of salt
1 teaspoon of ground black pepper
5 tablespoons of water

Wash your hands.

Use the electric blender to blend the chickpeas
until they are smooth.
Add the parsley and the onion to the
chickpeas in a bowl and mix.

Now add the spices and seasoning
(salt, pepper, chili, cumin and coriander)
and mix again.

Now add the egg and water and mix until the
mixture binds together.

Leave the mixture to rest for five minutes
while you tidy up.
Then wash your hands.

Now place a spoonful of the mixture on your hand and

Using the other hand roll into a small ball and place on a plate.

Keep doing this until you have used up all the mixture.

Now the balls are ready to be fried.

Ruemu

We hope you have enjoyed reading these poems. Now have a go at writing your own using these opening lines to get you started. Have fun!

My Garden of Earthly Delights

In my garden of earthly delights I shall put the warmth of a summer's day.

In my garden of earthly delights I shall put

_____

and

_____

In my garden of earthly delights I shall put

_____

and

_____

In my garden of earthly delights I shall put

_____

and

_____

In my garden of earthly delights I shall put

_____

and

_____

What's your problem? is a selection of poems by pupils and students who have attended Guy's Evelina Hospital School as inpatients or outpatients over the preceding months. There are also two other poems: one by a Mum of one of our pupils, one by a student nurse, just two of the many visitors the school welcomes regularly. There's even a DIY poem for you!

Guy's Evelina Hospital School is a Southwark LEA maintained Special School serving hospitalized pupils and young people aged between 2 and 19. Our work complements the provisions of two NHS trusts: Guy's and St. Thomas' and the South London and Maudsley. Our classrooms divide into Early Years, Primary, Secondary, Timbo (dialysis) and Adolescent Psychiatric (Snowsfields Unit and, for a period of eighteen months, Bloomfield Clinic). We also teach at bedside and offer home tuition for pupils with medical needs. We work with pupils from all over London, nationally and beyond. Our pupils' home schools are in the state and private sectors. Others may have college places. Some have neither school nor college places when they come to us. We have therefore perhaps one of the most comprehensive intakes of any school in the country! Each teaching area is represented in this book.

The Evelina Hospital School will be the new name for Guy's Evelina Hospital School from 2005, when the school expands to be based on two sites. The two sites are: the new Evelina Hospital, situated on the St. Thomas' Hospital site, to which the paediatric wards will move from Guy's, and the York Clinic of Guy's Hospital where the Snowsfields Adolescent Unit will remain.